I0762597

ANIMAL ALBUMS
THE
BEAR
FAMILY
BY GOLRIZ GOLKAR
eureka!
EUREKA!, AN IMPRINT OF BELLWETHER MEDIA BY FLUTTERBEE

eureka!

***Eureka!*** books turn real stories into unforgettable experiences. Clear, direct language and sharp, captivating imagery make it easy to follow your curiosity, one fascinating fact at a time. Your Eureka! moment awaits!

This edition first published in 2027 by Bellwether Media, Inc.



For information regarding permission, write to Bellwether Media, Inc., Attention: Permissions Department, 3500 American Blvd W, Suite 150, Bloomington, MN 55431.

Library of Congress Cataloging-in-Publication Data is available at www.loc.gov or upon request from the publisher.

ISBN: 9798898801298 (hardcover)
ISBN: 9798898802530 (ebook)

Editor: Rebecca Sabelko Series Designer: Jeff Kollock

Printed in the United States of America, North Mankato, MN.

# TABLE OF CONTENTS

# WHAT ARE BEARS?

Bears are mammals of the Ursidae family. There are eight species of bears and many more subspecies. Bears are found in North America, South America, Europe, and Asia. All bear species have ranges in the northern hemisphere. Only spectacled bears and sun bears are found south of the equator. Bears may live in forest, mountain, tundra, grassland, desert, and wetland habitats.

SUN BEAR ▶

▼ GIANT PANDA

## GREAT HEIGHTS

**The tallest recorded modern bear was a polar bear. It stood just over 11 feet (3.4 meters) tall on its hind legs. Prehistoric short-faced bears may have been around 12 feet (3.7 meters) tall.**

▲ POLAR BEAR

TAXONOMY CHART

Bears are large animals. Their legs and tails are short. They have a strong sense of smell. Many bear species are good swimmers and tree climbers.

ASIATIC BLACK BEAR

AMERICAN BLACK BEAR with cubs

# THE HISTORY OF BEARS

The first bears appeared around 23 million years ago. They evolved from doglike animals. These small bears ate plants and insects.

**ILLUSTRATION** of an early bear species

## EXTINCT BEARS

**Giant short-faced bears became extinct about 12,500 years ago. These bears likely died out because their large prey went extinct. They also had to compete with smaller, omnivorous bears.**

Bears moved around the world as Earth's land and climate changed. They adapted to different habitats. They became bigger. Their teeth allowed them to chew both plants and meat. Other adaptations helped many bear species survive over time. These include their thick fur and curved claws for hunting, foraging, and climbing. Females' ability to give birth to several cubs per litter helped the animals survive as well.

# EVOLUTIONARY EXCELLENCE

**SHOULDERS AND HUMP**
help bears run fast, forage for food, and take down prey

**TEETH**
sharp canine teeth help bears tear meat, and molars help them eat plants

**CURVED CLAWS**
help bears hunt, forage, and climb

**NOSE**
helps bears find food and sense danger through smell

# LIFE CYCLE

Adult bears mostly live alone. Males and females only meet to mate. Females often give birth in dens to two or three babies. Babies are called cubs. Cubs are born with their eyes and ears closed. They have little to no hair. They need their mother to survive.

▼**BEAR CUB** drinking mother's milk

**BEAR DEN**▲

Bear cubs drink their mother's milk. They grow fast. Their mother teaches them how to find food and stay safe from predators. Cubs stay with their mother for up to three years, depending on when the mother is ready to mate again.

## AVERAGE LIFE SPAN IN THE WILD

AROUND 20 YEARS

25 TO 30 YEARS

AROUND 10 YEARS

AROUND 15 YEARS

# BEAR LANGUAGE AND BEHAVIOR

## BODY LANGUAGE AND SOUNDS

Bears may wrestle or make clicking or grunting sounds to show they are content. They may flatten their ears and charge toward threats when they are scared. They also blow out air and clack their teeth.

**CLAW MARKS**
on a tree

## SCENT MARKING AND CLAWING

Bears rub their backsides against trees to leave a scent. They may claw or bite trees. These behaviors show their interest in mating and tell other bears where they have been.

## TORPOR

Bears enter a deep sleep state called torpor during winter. They may wake up easily if they sense danger. Females sometimes wake up to give birth.

**BROWN BEAR ▲**
**entering den for torpor**

### SLEEPY BEARS

**Bears can sleep more than six months without drinking, eating, or passing waste.**

# BEAR FAMILY TREE

▲ **GIANT PANDAS**
2 subspecies

▲ **POLAR BEARS**

Polar bears are the largest land animals on Earth that only eat meat.

▲ **SPECTACLED BEARS**

▲ **SLOTH BEARS**
2 subspecies

Sloth bears mark their territories by ripping bark off trees.

# URSIDAE

▲ **SUN BEARS**
2 subspecies

▲ **AMERICAN BLACK BEARS**
16 subspecies

Spirit bears are an American black bear subspecies. There are only about 400 spirit bears in the wild.

▲ **BROWN BEARS**
16 subspecies

Grizzly bears are a brown bear subspecies. They can run up to 35 miles (56 kilometers) per hour.

▲ **ASIATIC BLACK BEARS**
7 subspecies

# GIANT PANDAS

Giant pandas are vulnerable bears. Farming and deforestation have forced them out of their natural lowland habitat into mountainous areas.

## WHERE DO THEY LIVE?

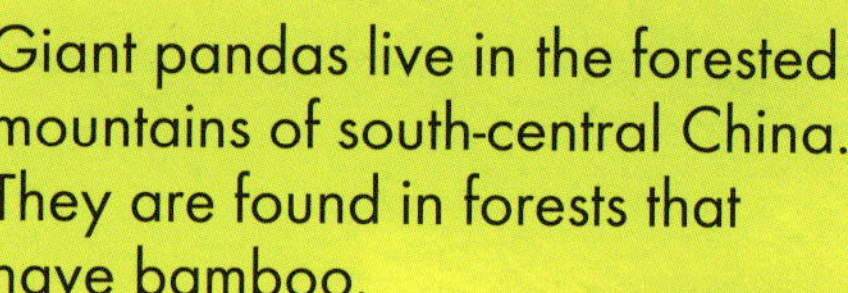

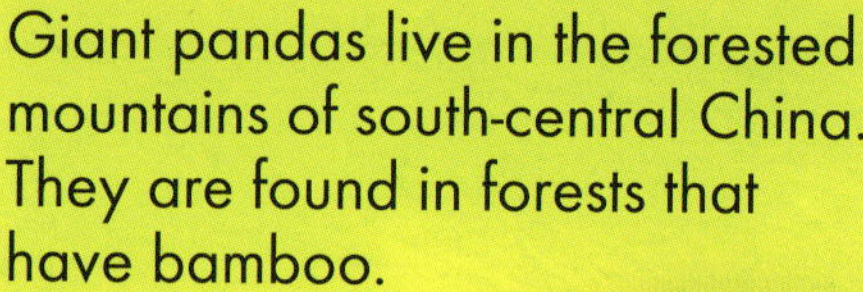

Giant pandas live in the forested mountains of south-central China. They are found in forests that have bamboo.

## DIET

These bears eat bamboo leaves, shoots, and stems. Pandas must eat at least 12 hours per day to get the amount of food they need.

## APPEARANCE

Their coats are white. Their legs, shoulders, ears, mouths, and eye areas are black. An extra wrist bone in their front paws acts as a thumb to help them grasp bamboo.

## FAMOUS GIANT PANDA

### Hua Hua

- **Location:**
  **The Chengdu Research Base of Giant Panda Breeding, Chengdu, Sichuan, China**
- **Famous for:**
  **Hua Hua receives millions of visitors every year. She has many followers on social media. Her face is often seen on billboards, posters, and gift items.**

## SIZE COMPARISON

**1,600LBS (726 kg)**

polar bear

**300LBS (136 kg)**

giant panda

**595LBS (270 kg)**

cinnamon bear

### TIME TO GO

**Giant pandas poop around 40 times per day.**

# SPECTACLED BEARS

Spectacled bears are named for the light markings around their eyes. Some look like they are wearing glasses! They are also called Andean bears.

## APPEARANCE

Spectacled bears are some of the smallest bears. They have round faces and short, wide snouts. Their thick coats are dark brown to black.

## VULNERABLE SPECIES

▼ SPECTACLED BEAR ▼
VULNERABLE

**THREATS**

habitat loss

hunting

climate change

**CONSERVATION EFFORTS ▼**

habitat protection

local education programs

hunting and trading bans

## WHERE DO THEY LIVE?

They mostly live in the dense forests of the Andes Mountains in South America. They are the only native bears on the continent.

### THE LAST OF ITS KIND

The spectacled bear is the last remaining species of the short-faced bear subfamily. They belong to a group of bears that first lived around 1.8 million years ago.

## SIZE COMPARISON

783LBS (355 kg)

Eurasian brown bear

340LBS (154 kg)

spectacled bear

551LBS (250 kg)

glacier bear

## DIET

Spectacled bears find food in trees and on the ground. They eat fruits, flowers, grasses, and plant bulbs. They also eat birds, rabbits, and rodents.

# POLAR BEARS

Polar bears are the largest bear species. They are fierce apex predators in their habitats.

## WHERE DO THEY LIVE?

Polar bears mostly live on sea ice in the Arctic region.

## VULNERABLE SPECIES

**POLAR BEAR**
**▼ VULNERABLE ▼**

**THREATS**

melting ice due to climate change

oil drilling

pollution

**CONSERVATION EFFORTS ▼**

educational programs to slow climate change

laws protecting them from hunting and habitat loss

## APPEARANCE

Polar bears have a thick layer of body fat. Their coats are warm and waterproof. Their fur is clear. They look white because of the way light bounces off their fur. Their large, slightly webbed paws act as paddles to help them swim.

### KEEPING FULL

**Polar bears can eat 100 pounds (45 kilograms) of seal blubber at once.**

## DIET

Polar bears mostly eat seal blubber. They wait at breathing holes for seals to come up for air. They grab seals from the water with their sharp teeth and claws.

## SIZE COMPARISON

| polar bear | Asiatic black bear | sloth bear |
|---|---|---|
| 1,600 LBS (726 kg) | 331 LBS (150 kg) | 310 LBS (141 kg) |

# SLOTH BEARS

Sloth bears are small, shaggy-haired bears. They are named for their sloth-like teeth and long, hooked claws. Their claws help them climb trees and dig for insects.

## DIET

Sloth bears use their claws to make a hole in termite or ant mounds. They put their lips around the hole and suck the insects into their mouths through a gap in their front teeth.

## VULNERABLE SPECIES

**SLOTH BEAR**
**▼ VULNERABLE ▼**

### THREATS

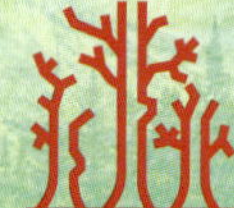
habitat loss due to deforestation

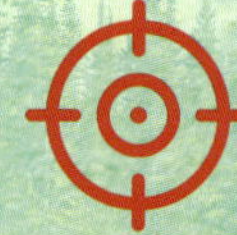
hunting

capture

### CONSERVATION EFFORTS ▼

habitat protection

hunting and trading bans

## WHERE DO THEY LIVE?

Sloth bears live in South Asia. They are found in grasslands, scrublands, and forests.

## SIZE COMPARISON

## APPEARANCE

These bears have black or brown fur and a white, V-shaped chest marking. Short, light-colored hair covers their long snouts.

# SUN BEARS

Sun bears are the smallest bear species. They are named after the golden patch on their chest. It looks like a rising sun.

## APPEARANCE

Sun bears are stocky with small ears and short, light-colored snouts. Their black coats have short, thick, coarse fur. It keeps them from overheating. It also protects them from rain and scratches from twigs.

## DIET

Sun bears rip open tree bark, beehives, and termite nests with their long, curved claws. They use their flexible snouts and long tongues to reach sap, honey, and insects.

## SIZE COMPARISON

**595LBS** (270 kg)

cinnamon bear

**300LBS** (136 kg)

giant panda

**150LBS** (68 kg)

sun bear

## FAMOUS SUN BEAR

### TSUYOSHI

- **Location:** Shunan, Yamaguchi, Japan

- **Famous for:** Tsuyoshi was a sun bear that lived at the Tokuyama Zoo in Shunan, Japan. He was known for throwing his arms up in the air in a frustrated pose when other bears took his food.

**SUN BEAR**
Range in the Wild

## WHERE DO THEY LIVE?

Sun bears live in the tropical lowland forests of Southeast Asia.

# EASTERN BLACK BEARS

Eastern black bears are one of the 16 American black bear subspecies.

**COMMON BEARS**

**American black bears are the most common bears in North America.**

## SIZE COMPARISON

| 1,600LBS (726 kg) | 441LBS (200 kg) | 340LBS (154 kg) |
|---|---|---|
| polar bear | eastern black bear | spectacled bear |

## DIET

They eat mostly tree bark, grasses, nuts, fruit, and honey. They search for invertebrates under rocks and in logs and dirt. These bears sometimes eat mice, rabbits, and fish.

## WHERE DO THEY LIVE?

American black bears are found in Canada, the United States, and Mexico. But eastern black bears live east of Montana, as far south as Texas, and in parts of Canada. Some live in Alaska. These bears roam woodlands and forested areas of swamps.

## APPEARANCE

Eastern black bears have stocky bodies. They have long, thick black fur and tan snouts. Their front claws are longer than their hind claws.

## RELATED SPECIES

### LOUISIANA BLACK BEAR

- **Range:** Louisiana and parts of southern Mississippi and eastern Texas
- **Known for:** These bears have a smaller body and narrower skull than other black bears. They almost disappeared due to habitat loss and hunting, but conservation programs have helped keep their population stable.

# CINNAMON BEARS

Cinnamon bears are an American black bear subspecies. They get their name from their light, cinnamon-colored coats.

## WHERE DO THEY LIVE?

These bears live in both forested lowland and mountainous areas. They roam the Rocky Mountains and parts of the western U.S. They also live in British Columbia and western Alberta, Canada.

## DIET

They eat mostly fruits, plants, and nuts. These bears also eat honey, insects, fish, and rodents.

## SIZE COMPARISON

| 1,500 LBS (680 kg) | 595 LBS (270 kg) | 150 LBS (68 kg) |
|---|---|---|
|  |  |  |
| Kodiak bear | cinnamon bear | sun bear |

## APPEARANCE

Cinnamon bears have brown or reddish-brown coats. Their foreheads are flatter than some other black bear subspecies. They have short, curved claws.

## FAMOUS CINNAMON BEAR

### MURPHY

**Location:**
ZooAmerica in Hershey, Pennsylvania

**Famous for:**
This cinnamon bear was first discovered approaching people's homes in search of food. He was taken to ZooAmerica. He was gentle with all the people he saw.

# SPIRIT BEARS

Spirit bears are an American black bear subspecies. These rare bears have genes that turn their coats white.

## WHERE DO THEY LIVE?

They live in the Great Bear Rainforest along British Columbia's north and central coasts in Canada.

## DIET

Spirit bears mostly eat fruits, nuts, plants, and insects. They prefer to eat salmon before their winter sleep. They often catch salmon by grabbing them with their mouths.

## SIZE COMPARISON

**805LBS** (365 kg)

spirit bear

**300LBS** (136 kg)

giant panda

**551LBS** (250 kg)

glacier bear

## FAMOUS SPIRIT BEAR

### MA'AH

- **Range:**
  Great Bear Rainforest, British Columbia, Canada

- **Famous for:**
  Ma'ah was a gentle female spirit bear whose name means "grandmother" in the Gitga'at language. She was often spotted looking for salmon. She was the oldest known spirit bear in the Great Bear Rainforest.

## CATCHING FISH

Spirit bears are more successful at catching fish than other black bear species. Scientists believe their white fur is harder for salmon to spot during the day.

## APPEARANCE

Like other black bear species, spirit bears are medium-sized. They have smooth, short-haired coats. They have rounded faces, brown eyes, and black noses. Their white claws are curved.

# GLACIER BEARS

Glacier bears are the rarest American black bears. Their silvery blue coats camouflage them in their icy habitat. Their coats protect them from predators such as brown bears and wolves.

## DIET

They use their claws to dig marmots, mice, and squirrels from burrows. They also eat salmon, shellfish, berries, and plants.

## APPEARANCE

These bears have a blue-black undercoat with long white to yellow outer hairs. These hairs have silver tips.

# WHERE DO THEY LIVE?

Glacier bears live in parts of western Canada and southeastern Alaska. They roam the coast, coastal mountains, and glacier-filled valleys.

= Range

**GLACIER BEAR**
Range in the Wild

## COLOR ADAPTATION

Scientists think glacier bears' blue coloring may have appeared during the Ice Age to help these bears blend in with the ice.

## SIZE COMPARISON

| 340 LBS (154 kg) | 331 LBS (150 kg) | 551 LBS (250 kg) |
|---|---|---|
|  |  |  |
| spectacled bear | Asiatic black bear | glacier bear |

## RELATED SPECIES

### VANCOUVER ISLAND BLACK BEAR

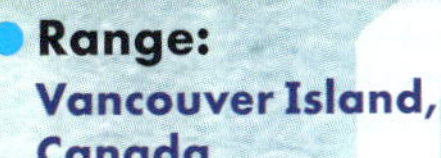

- **Range:** Vancouver Island, Canada
- **Known for:** These bears are a slightly bigger and darker black bear subspecies. There are around 10,000 individuals on the island, making it one of the most densely populated bear habitats on Earth. These bears are active during the day, unlike many black bear species.

# GRIZZLY BEARS

Grizzly bears are a subspecies of brown bears. They once lived throughout western North America. Human settlement greatly reduced their range.

GRIZZLY BEAR

Range in the Wild

## WHERE DO THEY LIVE?

Most grizzly bears live in Alaska and western Canada. Smaller populations are found in Wyoming, Idaho, Montana, and Washington. They thrive in tundra, grassland, and forest habitats far away from humans.

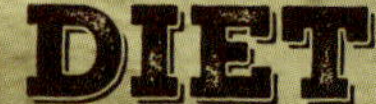


These bears are top predators. They hunt anything from rodents to moose. But they mostly eat fruits, nuts, leaves, and roots.

**Grizzly bears have large home ranges. They extend up to 600 square miles (1,554 square kilometers).**

## SIZE COMPARISON

**1,600LBS** (726 kg)

polar bear

grizzly bear

**441LBS** (200 kg)

eastern black bear

**FAMOUS GRIZZLY BEAR**

## GRIZZLY 399

- **Location:**
  Grand Teton National Park, Wyoming

- **Famous for:**
  Grizzly 399 was the most photographed grizzly in the world. She inspired conservation programs to work harder to protect these bears from human conflict and habitat loss.

## APPEARANCE

These bears have short, rounded ears and humped shoulders. Their coats range from light tan to dark brown. Their long outer guard hairs often have silver or golden tips.

# KODIAK BEARS

Kodiak bears are a brown bear subspecies. They are among the largest bears on Earth.

## APPEARANCE

Kodiak bears have light to dark brown coats. They have round ears and large shoulder humps. Their claws can be up to 6 inches (15 centimeters) long.

### FAMOUS KODIAK BEAR

**BART THE BEAR**

- **Location:** born at the Baltimore Zoo, Maryland
- **Famous for:** Bart the Bear was an actor in many movies and TV shows. He was known for his gentle nature and stunts.

## DIET

These bears eat any food they can find. They mostly eat berries, plants, and salmon. They also roam beaches to search for carrion.

## SIZE COMPARISON

| 1,500 LBS (680 kg) | 783 LBS (355 kg) | 150 LBS (68 kg) |
|---|---|---|
|  |  |  |
| Kodiak bear | Eurasian brown bear | sun bear |

## WHERE DO THEY LIVE?

Kodiak bears live in Alaska's Kodiak Archipelago. They adapt well to different habitats, including tundra, forests, mountains, and salt marshes.

# EURASIAN BROWN BEARS

Eurasian brown bears once roamed much of Europe and northwestern Asia. Their range is much smaller today due to habitat loss and hunting.

## WHERE DO THEY LIVE?

Eurasian brown bears mostly live in Russia. Populations also live in wooded mountains throughout other parts of Europe.

## DIET

These bears eat mostly fruits, plants, nuts, and insects. Sometimes they eat fish and carrion.

# SIZE COMPARISON

| 1,323 LBS (600 kg) | 783 LBS (355 kg) | 551 LBS (250 kg) |
|---|---|---|
| Ussuri brown bear | Eurasian brown bear | glacier bear |

# APPEARANCE

These bears have wide heads, long snouts, and small, round ears. They have humped shoulders. Most have thick, brown coats. But coat colors can range from white to almost black.

## RELATED SPECIES

### KAMCHATKA BROWN BEAR

- **Range:** Kamchatka Peninsula, Russia
- **Known for:** These bears are the largest Eurasian brown bear subspecies. They can be nearly 8 feet (2.4 meters) tall and can weigh 1,543 pounds (700 kilograms).

# USSURI BROWN BEARS

Ussuri brown bears are named after the Ussuri River. This river is between China and Russia. These bears are also known as black grizzly bears.

## DIET

These bears eat fish, mammals, birds, insects, berries, and nuts. They may also feed on carrion.

## APPEARANCE

Ussuri brown bears are usually dark brown but may be black. They have long skulls, low foreheads, and long snouts.

## WHERE DO THEY LIVE?

Ussuri brown bears are found in parts of China, Japan, and Russia. They live in forests, mountains, and coastal areas.

## SIZE COMPARISON

**1,323LBS** (600 kg)

Ussuri brown bear

**1,600LBS** (726 kg)

polar bear

**800LBS** (363 kg)

grizzly bear

## FAMOUS USSURI BROWN BEAR

### KESAGAKE

**Location:**
Sankebetsu, Hokkaido, Japan

**Famous for:**
This giant bear woke early in the winter of 1915. It took the lives of seven humans over several days. The attack was the deadliest bear attack in Japan's history.

# ASIATIC BLACK BEARS

- Asiatic black bears are often called moon bears. They are known for the white moon-shaped patch on their chest.

## DIET

Asiatic black bears mostly eat fruits and roots. They use their strong sense of smell to find insects and grubs up to 3 feet (1 meter) underground. They may also eat mammals, carrion, and tree bark.

## VULNERABLE SPECIES

**HIMALAYAN BLACK BEAR**
**▼ VULNERABLE ▼**

THREATS

habitat loss

hunting

habitat protection

anti-hunting efforts

# WHERE DO THEY LIVE?

Asiatic black bears thrive in thick, moist forested mountains throughout parts of Asia.

## APPEARANCE

These bears have black coats, pale snouts, and a shaggy mane around their faces. Their strong forearms and short, curved claws help them climb.

## SIZE COMPARISON

| 1,500 LBS (680 kg) | 800 LBS (363 kg) | 331 LBS (150 kg) |
| --- | --- | --- |
| Kodiak bear | grizzly bear | Asiatic black bear |

# BEARS AND PEOPLE

Bears have had a strong connection to humans for thousands of years. Many cultures honor bears as strong, wise, and brave animals. Bears are often shown as frightening creatures in movies, art, books, and TV. But they are also popular children's toys and shown as gentle and loving in many cartoons.

OIL DRILLING ▼

Bears face many threats due to human behaviors. Habitat loss is a major problem that affects many species. Climate change, pollution, oil drilling, and land development are forcing bears out of their native habitats. Hunting threatens many species too.

## FOLKLORE PROFILE

**NAME:**

**URSA MAJOR AND URSA MINOR**

**ORIGIN:**

**ANCIENT ROME**

**FAMOUS FOR:**

**Ursa Major was a beautiful maiden turned into a bear by Juno, the god Jupiter's jealous wife. Her son Arcas was turned into a bear named Ursa Minor. Jupiter threw them both into the sky to live peacefully and safely among the stars. They are now constellations.**

Many organizations are working to protect bears. Some work to pass laws that ban hunting, reduce pollution, and stop other human behaviors that cause climate change. Educational programs teach people how to live peacefully with bears. Some bears are cared for at zoos and studied at national parks.

SUN BEAR CONSERVATION CENTER ▼

▼ BEAR SANCTUARY

Everyone can help bears by pushing governments to pass laws that protect bear habitats and fight climate change. People can respect bears' natural habitats by throwing trash away responsibly and giving bears their space. By working together, people can give bears a long and healthy future!

# GLOSSARY

**adapted**—changed over a period of time

**archipelago**—a group of islands

**camouflage**—to blend in with surroundings

**carrion**—the rotting meat of a dead animal

**climate**—the usual temperature, precipitation, and other weather conditions of an area

**climate change**—a human-caused process in which Earth's average weather changes over a long period of time

**cultures**—the beliefs, arts, and ways of life in a place or society

**deforestation**—the act of cutting down a wide area of trees

**equator**—the imaginary line around the center of Earth

**evolved**—changed from one form into a new form

**genes**—tiny instructions inside cells that carry information about traits that are passed down from parents to their children

**guard hairs**—long, thick hairs on the outside of a bear's coat

**habitats**—natural homes of plants and animals

**hemisphere**—a half of the earth

**invertebrates**—animals without backbones

**mammals**—warm-blooded animals that have backbones and feed their young milk

**native**—originally from a certain place

**pollution**—substances that make the earth dirty or unsafe; pollution usually comes from humans' actions.

**rainforest**—a thick, green forest that receives a lot of rain

**scrublands**—dry lands that have mostly low plants and few trees

**snouts**—the noses and mouths of some animals

**species**—groups of living things that are alike and can reproduce with one another; subspecies are particular types of animals that exist within a species.

**threats**—actions or animals that can cause harm

**tundra**—a flat treeless area where the ground is always frozen

**vulnerable**—at risk of becoming endangered

## WRITE ABOUT IT!

- What bear species would you like to learn more about? **Why?**
- What bear behavior do you think is the most interesting? **Why?**
- **What** changes can you make in your life that could help keep bears and their habitats safe?

## ALSO CHECK OUT

ANIMAL ALBUMS THE SNAKE FAMILY eureka!

ANIMAL ALBUMS THE CAT FAMILY eureka!

ANIMAL ALBUMS SHARK FAMILY eureka!

# INDEX





The images in this book are reproduced through the courtesy of: Abid Ali, front cover, p. 1; woopics, front cover, p. 1; Adilson, front cover, pp. 1, 12 (spectacled); Sangur, front cover, p. 1; Zakharov Evgeniy, front cover, p. 1; VarnakovR, front cover, p. 1; Ralph Lear, pp. 3, 16, 17 (left); Trixy, p. 3; Sabrina Herrmann, p. 4 (top); Hung Chung Chih, p. 4 (panda); KrisGrabiec, p. 4 (polar); Erik Mandre, pp. 5, 8; Danita Delimont, p. 5 (left); Anan Kaewkhammul, p. 5 (right); Roger Witter/ Wikimedia Commons, p. 6 (top); mtatman, p. 6 (middle); Chris Woodrich/ Wikimedia Commons, p. 6 (fun fact); Praxis Creative, p. 6 (bottom); Friedrich, p. 7 (top); Stefany Hedman, p. 7 (left); Patrick Rolands, p. 7 (right); winterdog, p. 8 (top); K Quinn Ferris, p. 8 (cub); Rob Schultz, p. 8 (den); Uryadnikov Sergey, p. 9; Jonathan Steele, p. 9 (grizzly); andreanita, p. 9 (polar); Caleb, p. 9 (black); LP2 Studio, p. 9 (panda); steflas, p. 10 (top); Justgoexplore, p. 10 (marks); Veljko Klari , p. 10; Nature Picture Library/ Alamy Stock Photo, p. 11 (left); PhotoSpirit, p. 11 (middle); creativenature.nl, pp. 11 (right), 36 (top); imageBROKER.com GmbH & Co. KG/ Alamy Stock Photo, p. 11; SIMANG, p. 12 (panda); Rixie, p. 12 (polar); gudkovandrey, p. 12 (sloth); Natalia, p. 13 (sun); Thomas J Mitchell, p. 13 (spirit); Michael, p. 13 (grizzly); Volodymyr Burdiak, pp. 13 (Asiatic), 40 (top, middle); Foreverhappy, p. 14 (top); Curioso. Photography, p. 14 (left); Daniel Ferryanto, p. 14 (right); LP2Studio, p. 15 (top); Atta7788, p. 15; Ahlan, p. 16 (main); Christian Musat, p. 16 (middle); Stef Bennett, p. 16 (left); PhotocechCZ, pp. 17 (right), 22 (top); Danica Chang, p. 17 (bottom); Don Landwehrle, p. 18 (top, right); David, p. 18 (left); imageBROKER.com, p. 19 (left); chbaum, p. 19 (right); Mario Hoppmann, p. 19 (middle); Nadine, p. 19 (main); Gabrielle, p. 19 (bottom); Holly S Cannon, p. 20 (top); photocech, p. 20 (termite); AdrianZeus, p. 20 (left); Martin Mecnarowski, p. 20 (right, bottom); Spiks, p. 21 (left); Andrea Izzotti, p. 21 (right); ManoStudioArt, pp. 21, 24 (main), 34; MrPreecha, p. 22 (middle); jmubalde, p. 22 (bottom); anankkml, pp. 22, 41; MIIA, p. 23 (left); Bornean Sun Bear Conservation Centre/ Wikimedia Commons, p. 23 (middle); Nakornthai, p. 23 (right); Ben McMurtray, pp. 24 (top), 25; KQ Ferris, p. 24 (left); Paul, p. 24 (right); Asp3/ Wirestock Creators, p. 25 (profile); Bruce Montagne/ Dembinsky Photo Associates/ Alamy Stock Photo, p. 26 (top); imaton, p. 26; Menno Schaefer, p. 26 (bottom); Dennis, p. 27 (top); kellyvandellen, p. 27 (middle); Amy, p. 27 (bottom); Richard Seeley, pp. 28 (all), 29 (profile); kongsak sumano, p. 29 (fun fact, main); Hal Photography, p. 29 (left); Scott Canning, p. 29 (right); Image Source Limited/ Alamy Stock Photo, pp. 30 (top, main), 31; Mirko Ropelato, p. 30 (marmot); Cristian H. Gomez, p. 30 (shellfish); National Parks Service/ Wikimedia Commons, p. 31 (top); Don Laidlaw, p. 31 (profile); Robert Harding Video, p. 32 (top); Roger, p. 32 (middle); H. Mark Weidman Photography/ Alamy Stock Photo, p. 32 (bottom); Harry Collins Photography, p. 33 (top); GrandTetonNPS/ Wikimedia Commons, p. 33 (profile); Robert McGouey/ Wildlife/ Alamy Stock Photo, p. 33 (bottom); Marigold, p. 33; Mark A. McCaffrey, pp. 34 (top), 35 (top); Jon Freeman Online USA Inc/ Wikimedia Commons, p. 34 (profile); USFWSAlaska/ Wikimedia Commons, pp. 34 (bottom), 35 (bottom); Lisa Hupp/ USFWS/ Wikimedia Commons, p. 35 (middle); Giedriius, pp. 36 (left), 37 (bottom); udmer Zwerver, p. 36 (right); Robert F. Tobler/ Wikimedia Commons, p. 37 (profile); Charles J. Sharp/ Wikimedia Commons, p. 37 (middle); Sergey Uryadnikov, p. 37; Frank Fichtmueller, p. 38 (top); Godimus Michel, p. 38 (left); Nathan Ruser/ Wikimedia Commons, p. 38 (middle); Choups/ Alamy Stock Photo, p. 38 (right); bryan.../ Wikimedia Commons, p. 38; , p. 39; Babi Hijau/ Wikimedia Commons, p. 39 (profile); Anan Kaewkhammul/ Alamy Stock Photo, p. 40; flowcomm/ Wikimedia Commons, p. 40 (left); Shiv's fotografia, p. 40 (right); Hari Prema, p. 40 (bottom); Samsul Huda Patgiri, p. 41 (top); teekayu, p. 41 (bottom); Aleksandr Dyskin, p. 42 (top); Daderot/ Wikimedia Commons, p. 42 (middle); steheap, p. 42 (left); National Agricultural Library/ Wikimedia Commons, p. 42 (right); / Wikimedia Commons, p. 42; Vladimir Endovitskiy, p. 43 (top); adamikarl, p. 43 (habitat); Sidney Hall/ Wikimedia Commons, p. 43 (middle); avvapanf Photo, p. 43 (bottom); CEphoto, Uwe Aranas/ Wikimedia Commons, p. 44 (top); Orlando Sentinel/ Getty Images, pp. 44 (middle), 45 (top); MIHAI BARBU/ Getty Images, p. 44; VCG/ Getty Images, p. 44 (left); Ari, p. 44 (right); CGN089, p. 45 (middle); stativius, p. 45 (left); FREDERIC J. BROWN/ Getty Images, p. 45 (right).